ZAYNA'S TIGER DAY

Written by Reba Khatun
Illustrated by Debasmita Dasgupta

OXFORD
UNIVERSITY PRESS

Words to look out for ...

attentive (adjective)

listening or watching carefully

continual (adjective)

happening repeatedly

devise (verb)
devises, devising, devised

To devise a plan or idea is to think it up.

fundamental (adjective)

very important

incident (noun)

something that happens, usually something bad or strange

omit (verb)
omits, omitting, omitted

To omit someone or something is to leave them out.

reputation (noun)

what most people say or think about someone or something

sincere (adjective)
sincerer, sincerest

You are being sincere when you mean what you say and express your true feelings.

Chapter 1

'Hi, Zaynab,' said Summer. My best friend came up to me at our table in the classroom.

Before I could answer, our teacher appeared beside us.

'Good morning, Mr Okonjo,' Summer said, passing her radio aid microphone to him.

Mr Okonjo hung it around his neck. 'Are you both having a good morning?' he asked.

'Yes, Mr Okonjo,' we replied at the same time.

Mr Okonjo clapped his hands and the classroom went quiet. 'Today, we have baking, PE, and we need to finish our "Save our favourite animal" projects. Remember, your families will be seeing them at our charity event and bake sale after school.'

I leaned over to speak to Summer, but Mr Okonjo saw me.

'Zaynab!' he said. 'How is your animal project with Summer going? Could you tell the class about it?'

'Oh no,' I thought, feeling nervous. Summer gave me an encouraging smile.

'Our project is about Bengal tigers,' I said slowly. 'There are 4500 Bengal tigers left in the world.'

'Wow, that's a lot of tigers!' said Layla.

My project book crashed to the floor. 'No!' I exclaimed. 'That's not a lot! Not compared to how many tigers there used to be.'

I turned to Mr Okonjo and asked, 'Can I try something?'

Mr Okonjo sat on the edge of his desk. 'Sure,' he said.

I looked at the calculations in my project book.

'There are 30 children in class today,' I said. 'Each child represents 3000 tigers. Altogether we make up 90 000 tigers. That's about the number of tigers that were alive in the wild 100 years ago. However ...'

I paused to make sure everyone was listening and attentive.

If you are attentive, you are listening or watching carefully.

'There are fewer tigers now because they have been hunted and their habitats have been destroyed,' I continued. 'I'm going to show you how much the number of tigers has gone down.'

I tapped Abdullah, Summer, David and Iris on the shoulders. 'If I tap both your shoulders, please go over to Mr Okonjo. It means that we've lost 3000 tigers.'

There were gasps. I tapped the shoulders of the people at another two tables.

'That's half the tigers gone!' Adam cried.

I dashed around the classroom, tapping almost everyone's shoulders. I stopped in front of Harpreet and tapped her on one shoulder.

'So half my tigers are gone?' asked Harpreet.

I nodded. 'My tigers and half of Harpreet's make up the four-and-a-half thousand tigers left in the wild today.'

I pointed to all the children by Mr Okonjo. 'This is how many more tigers there *used* to be.'

Mr Okonjo nodded, clearly impressed. 'That was a very interesting speech and I can tell you care about this. Thank you, Zaynab. Now, I would like everyone to work on yesterday's creative writing piece.'

Chapter 2

After break, Mr Okonjo had a big white chef's hat on.

'Can we make jelly?' asked Summer. 'Strawberry is my favourite.'

'No, we're making cupcakes to sell at the bake sale this afternoon. It's important to get them right! Be sure not to omit any ingredients.'

To omit someone or something is to leave them out.

I fished in my bag for the egg carton. It was soggy. When I opened it, I saw that all my eggs had great big cracks down them.

Then Summer knocked into the table by accident, sending my eggs crashing to the floor!

'Sorry,' said Summer, looking bashful.

'I wanted to make fabulous cupcakes to show Mum and Nani,' I muttered.

Harpreet and David went around putting bun trays and cupcake cases on the tables.

Mr Okonjo followed with scales and spoons. When he reached our table, he stepped on some spilt egg. He went sliding across the room like he was ice-skating!

'Everyone, please!' called Mr Okonjo. 'I could have broken my neck. To avoid a major incident, let me know immediately if you drop something.'

'Sorry, Mr Okonjo,' I sighed.

I scooped the remaining eggs from the carton into the mixing bowl, trying to leave out the eggshells.

An incident is something that happens, usually bad or strange.

Quite a few pieces of shell fell in and no matter how hard I tried, I couldn't get them out. I decided to crush them into tiny pieces. A few crunchy bits would surely not be noticed!

As Abdullah finished mixing in the flour, I put the cases into the bun tray.

I tried spooning the cake mixture into the cases. But more of it ended up on the tray and down the sides of the cases than inside them!

'You're wasting our mixture,' moaned Neil.

'No, I'm not,' I grumbled. However, I couldn't ignore the fact that there was more mixture outside the cases than inside.

'Don't worry,' said Mr Okonjo with a sincere smile. 'Zaynab, put your tray on the side. The teaching assistants will be baking all the cupcakes later.'

He put his hands on his hips and surveyed the room. It was a mess. 'Now let's tidy this classroom before assembly,' he said.

You are being sincere when you mean what you say and express your true feelings.

Chapter 3

When the teaching assistants brought the cupcakes into class after lunch, my stomach dropped. Our cupcakes were as flat as pancakes and the cake mixture on the sides was burnt.

'Nice,' muttered Abdullah, with a face like a fish.

'Just great,' huffed Neil, curling up his fists.

'No one will want these,' said Summer, crossing her arms sadly.

'I'm sure they will taste great,' said Mr Okonjo, though he stopped smiling when he actually saw our cupcakes. 'Time to finish off your decorations.'

Summer and I added the final touches to our poster. We finished connecting the orange triangles for the bunting before our PE lesson started.

At the end of the day, Mr Okonjo clapped to get our attention. 'It's time. Remember that you are representing our school and its reputation. Teach people about animals, raise money, and have fun!'

I grabbed our cupcakes and project book. Summer bundled up the bunting and poster and followed me out of the classroom.

Someone or something's reputation is what most people say or think about them.

Mr Okonjo caught up with us before we reached the playground. He placed Summer's microphone around my neck. 'That's so Summer can hear you over the noise out here,' he said.

'Thank you,' I called as we walked towards the school field. Our stall was in the far corner. Would anyone even notice us there?

I hung up our poster on the wall behind us.

Summer stuck the bunting along the edge of the table.

Our stall looked empty. It only had our flat cupcakes on one side and our project books on the other side.

'Is it enough?' I wondered.

Next to us, Layla had balloons and an enormous banner behind her table that said, 'WE LOVE PUPPIES!' She even had a pile of badges to give away.

'Sabrina's brought her kittens!' gasped Summer. I looked over to see three adorable tabby kittens trying to climb out of their box.

'How are we going to compete with that?' I thought, miserably. We had no free things to attract people to our stall.

'It's not fair. It's not like we can bring a tiger in,' I grumbled to myself.

Summer heard me. She shrugged.

Chapter 4

Suddenly Summer's jaw dropped open and her hand shook as she pointed behind me.

David was walking on to the school field holding the reins of a pony. A real, live, walking, neighing pony.

My day was getting worse by the minute. Everyone's stall was turning out to be better than ours.

A crowd of family members wandered into the playground.

I spotted Mum and Nani, and waved them over to our stall.

Mum rushed up to me and hugged me, before tidying my hair and smoothing down my school uniform. 'Did you have a good day?' she asked.

'Yes,' I said, trying to sound sincere.

Nani gave me a hug. She smelled of jasmine oil.

You are being sincere when you mean what you say and express your true feelings.

'What can we do to help?' asked Nani, licking her finger and scrubbing at my face.

I panicked. I didn't want them around all afternoon. 'Nothing. Why don't you go and check out the competition?' The last word stuck in my throat.

No other parent stopped by to visit our stall or talk to us.

Finally, Layla's mum hovered around, looking at our stall.

'How nice,' she said as she flicked through my project book.

I didn't know what to say. She gave me half a smile and fifty pence, and left.

'My mind went totally blank. Sorry,' said Summer, pulling a sad face.

I tried not to get upset. After all, I was the expert, but I hadn't been able to speak. I had let us both down. Summer wanted to do the stall on her pet rabbit but I had convinced her not to.

A large crowd of parents stood around Neil and his pet lizard, listening to how he took care of it.

I glanced at my watch. We only had forty minutes left!

'I'm bored,' yawned Summer. When she saw tears in my eyes she said, 'Tell me why you wanted to do our project on tigers.'

I forgot Summer didn't know. 'When Nani was younger, she told me she met a tiger,' I said.

Summer's hands flew up to her mouth. 'What?'

'She told me that when she was young, many, many years ago, she had no cares in the world,' I went on, remembering how Nani had told me the story. 'She played out all day under the sun with her cousins. That is, until the day the tiger turned up in her village in Bangladesh.'

'What happened?' squealed Summer.

'Nani and her cousins discovered a tiger on the roof of the cow shed. Luckily, the cows were in the field. The tiger wasn't fully grown. She was sure it looked her in the eyes,' I said.

'No way!' shouted Summer, startling a parent walking past. We looked at each other and giggled.

'How did it get there?' asked Summer.
'The tiger's home was thousands of miles away. It's a mystery how it ended up in the village. Even if it did walk all that way it would have taken months. People would have seen it along the way and stopped it,' I said.

'Before Nani could devise a plan, the other children started screaming. "Tiger! Tiger!" they shouted. The grown-ups came running and …'

'They captured the tiger,' guessed Summer.

'No. They killed it,' I whispered, my voice trembling.

'Oh.' Summer's mouth fell into an O shape. 'But why?'

'The adults were scared the tiger would return to hurt them. Tigers can be really dangerous. They can hurt people or farm animals, especially if they are hungry,' I explained.

To devise a plan or idea is to think it up.

'Nani and her cousins were very upset,' I went on. I was feeling very upset myself. It wasn't the adults' fault, but it wasn't the tiger's fault either. Tears fell down my own face like a waterfall.

'Nani told me that in that moment, she promised herself and the tiger that she would do all she could to protect its species.'

I wiped my tears away. 'Nani educated her family, and then her village. She helped set up a Tiger Protection Team for the nearby villages too.'

'That's why you chose tigers,' said Summer. I nodded.

'That's why I love them. They are magnificent and beautiful and need our help. I wanted to help them so much …'

Chapter 5

Summer drummed her fingers on the stall, gazing around the playground. She suddenly clasped her hands to her chest. 'I have an idea! To make our stall a success, would you repeat your classroom demonstration?'

The thought of talking to so many strangers made my stomach flip over.

Then I thought about Nani and all the tigers she'd rescued.

I nodded. 'Yes.'

The word was barely out of my mouth when Summer darted across the playground.

'Where are you going?' I shouted.

Summer didn't hear me. I sighed. What plan had Summer devised?

To devise a plan or idea is to think it up.

There was nothing I could do but wait. Not a single parent stopped at our stall. I spotted Mum and Nani fussing over Sabrina's kittens.

There were <u>continual</u> exclamations from people who saw the pony.

Finally, Summer returned, struggling with a large cardboard box.

I helped her carry the box to our stall.

If something is <u>continual</u>, it is happening repeatedly.

'What's in here?' I peeked inside.

A balloon escaped from the box. Summer caught the tail of the ribbon before it disappeared into the sky. She grabbed a few more balloons from the box and tied them to the table.

'Remember the reading challenge from last week?' Summer asked.

'Yes,' I said. 'It was "Wild About Reading". The library was decorated like a jungle.'

The box contained plastic animal models, a tiger mask and a large toy tiger. I knew Summer's plan! We could use them to dress up our stall.

Mr Okonjo appeared with a megaphone. 'As requested, Summer.'

Summer handed me the mask. 'Ready?'

Chapter 6

I took a deep breath, before nodding and putting on the tiger mask.

Summer switched on the megaphone. Feedback screeched out and she pulled a face. She leaned over and muted the microphone that was hanging around my neck.

'Roll up, roll up! Gather round to witness a most incredible thing!' shouted Summer.

Everyone stopped what they were doing.

I took another deep breath and swapped places with Summer. 'Our project is "Save the tigers",' I said into the megaphone. 'Though I couldn't bring one in, of course!'

People chuckled at this idea. I suddenly felt more confident.

'I want to show how important my charity is. Can I have 30 adults to help, please?' I asked.

Mr Okonjo, Mum and Nani volunteered. Soon I had all the adults I needed. I was ready to repeat my demonstration.

'Each adult represents 3000 tigers. All together, they show how many Bengal tigers there were 100 years ago,' I said.

'Since then, this number has been reduced because tigers' habitat has been destroyed and they have been hunted,' I continued. 'When I tap your arm, please move back into the crowd. The tigers that you represent have gone.'

I ran down the line, tapping every single adult on the arm, until I came to Mum and Nani.

Then I asked Mum to kneel down.

'Nani and half my mum represent the 4500 tigers in the wild today,' I said.

I lowered the megaphone and saw that everyone's mouths were open. I knew I had helped them understand how I felt about tigers.

Nani added, 'Our charity is fundamental in making sure that tigers in Bangladesh have enough land, so they don't wander into villages.'

If something is fundamental, it is very important.

A parent came to our stall and gave me a five-pound note. I gave her a cupcake.

She hesitated briefly before taking a nibble. 'It's buttery and sweet.'

My smile vanished when I heard a crunch. Our eyes locked.

'Oh, and crunchy! Fabulous!' she said with a wink.

Before we knew it, all the cupcakes had gone. Next to the plate was a big pile of coins and notes.

My heart filled with happiness. I couldn't wait to send the money to Nani's charity.

I gazed out into the crowd and caught Nani's gaze. She smiled, and her smile made me feel as proud as a tiger.